AWESOME
JOKES

FOR 8 YEAR OLDS

SILLY JOKES FOR KIDS AGED 8

What do you call cheese that does not belong to you?

a. Nacho cheese!

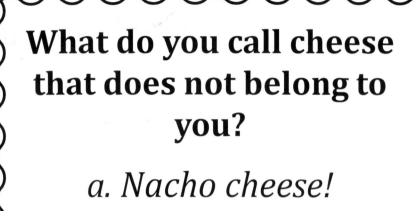

Knock knock.
a. Who's there?
b. Amish.
c. Amish who?
d. You look like a person, not a shoe!

Knock knock.

a. Who's there?

b. Canoe.

c. Canoe who?

**d. Canoe open the door?
It's raining!**

What should you do when you see a spaceman?

a. Park the car, man.

Knock knock.
a. Who's there?
b. Yah.
c. Yah who?
c. I'm a Bing user, actually.

Knock knock.
a. Who's there?
b. Isabel.
c. Isabel who?
**d. Isabel working,
I didn't hear it!**

What do bees use to fix their hair?

a. Honey combs!

Knock knock.
a. Who's there?
b. Justin
c. Justin who?
d. Justin the area and I thought I'd come by for a visit.

What do you call a girl who reads a lot?

a. Paige.

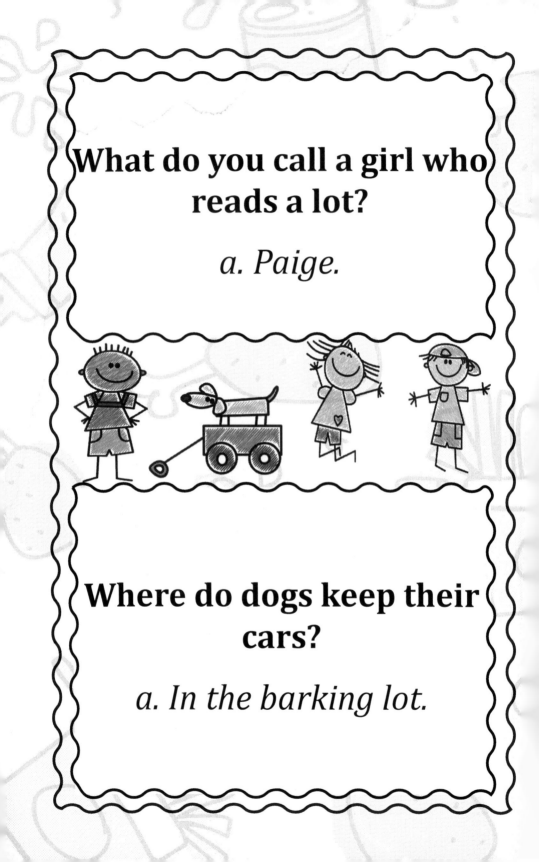

Where do dogs keep their cars?

a. In the barking lot.

What did the bee say when he finally met his pen pal?

a. Hive bee-n dying to meet you!

Why are barbers so quick?

a. Because they know short cuts.

Knock knock.
a. Who's there?
b. Purple.
c. Purple who?
d. Knock knock.
e. Who's there?
g. Purple who?
f. Purple.
h. Knock knock.
i. Who's there?
j. Orange.
k. Orange who?
l. Orange you glad I didn't say purple?

Why was six afraid to go near 7?

a. Because 7 ate 9!

What do you call a man with a sunburn?

a. Ray.

Knock knock.
a. Who's there?
b. Robins say.
c. Robins say who?
d. No, that's what owls say!

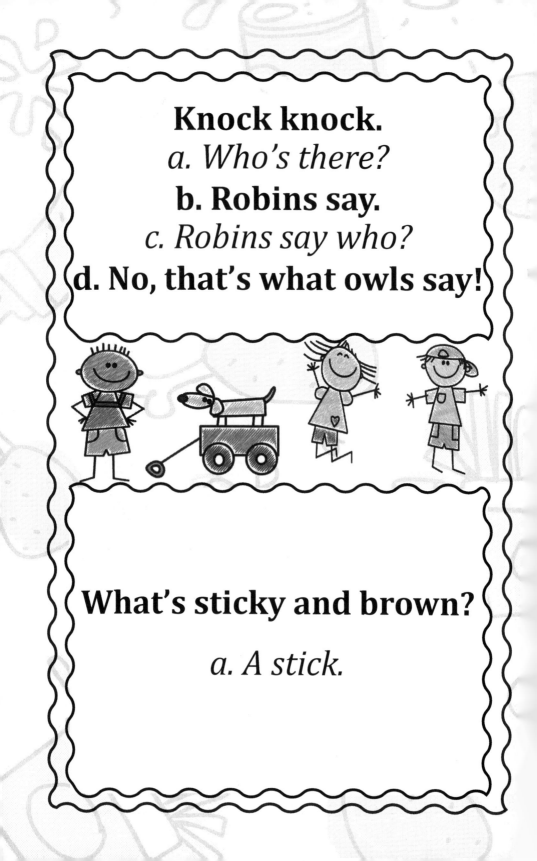

What's sticky and brown?

a. A stick.

Why does it take forever to cut the grass?

a. Because it's so lawn!

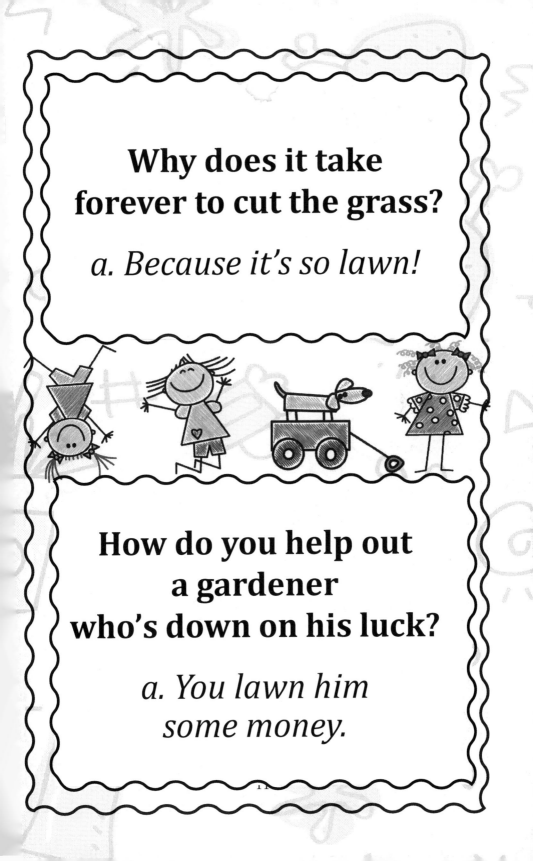

How do you help out a gardener who's down on his luck?

a. You lawn him some money.

My dad thinks I'm bright!

a. How do you know?

b. Because he calls me sun.

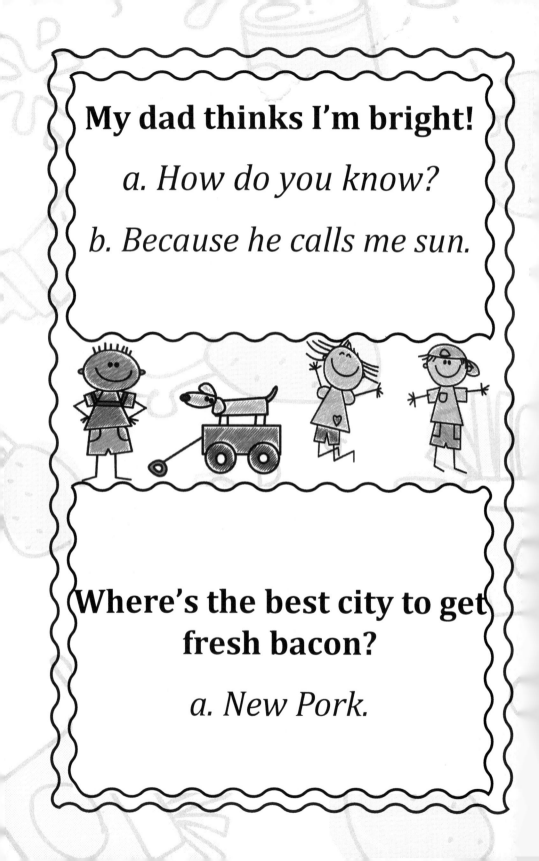

Where's the best city to get fresh bacon?

a. New Pork.

Why was the dragon out of a job?

a. Because he got fired.

What do you call someone who is good at drawing organs?

a. A heartist.

Where do you go to by novels about deer?

a. To the buckstore.

What is a clock's favorite season?

a. Spring!

What do you call someone who's good at getting apples out of barrels?

a. Bob.

Knock knock.
a. Who's there?
b. Wheel.
c. Wheel who?
d. Wheel be leaving soon if you don't open this door.

What kind of tree is from the future?

a. A "will"ow.

What is the most musical kind of paper?

a. Rapping paper.

What is a boxer's favorite office tool?

a. A three whole puncher.

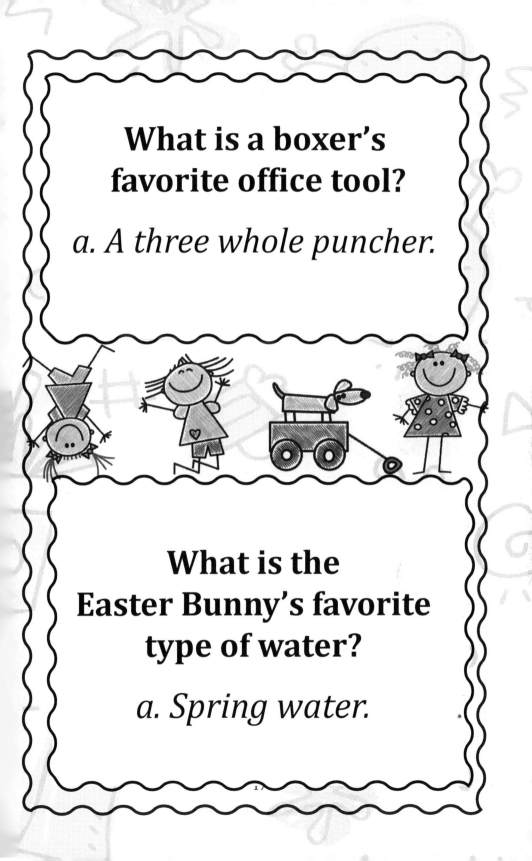

What is the Easter Bunny's favorite type of water?

a. Spring water.

How do you contact a crow?

a. You caw it.

What do you call a man who steals things?

a. Robert.

What kind of metal gets taken the most?

a. Steel.

What do you call a smelly computer?

a. A com-pee-yew-ter.

What's the smelliest body part?

a. The nose.

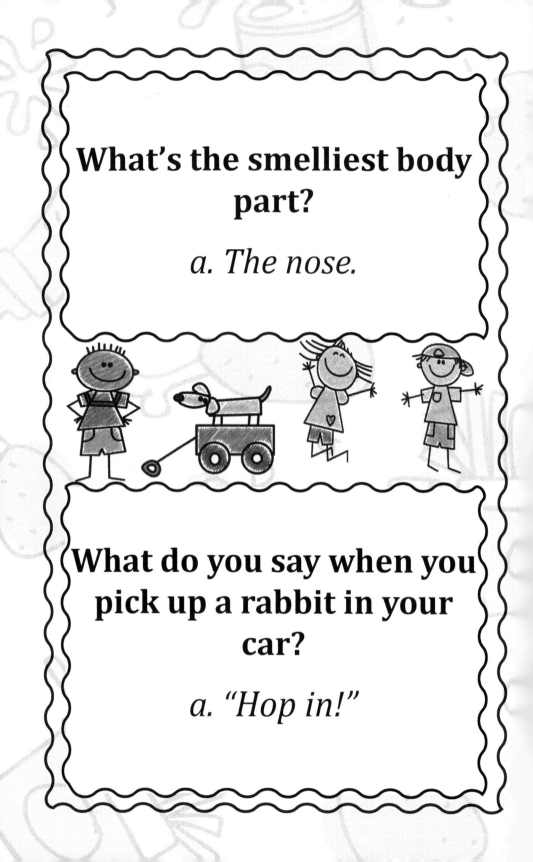

What do you say when you pick up a rabbit in your car?

a. "Hop in!"

What kind of table will get you wet?

a. A pool table.

Why did the fish have to change his sheets?

a. Because he dried the bed.

Why are quarry workers so young?

a. Because they are all miners.

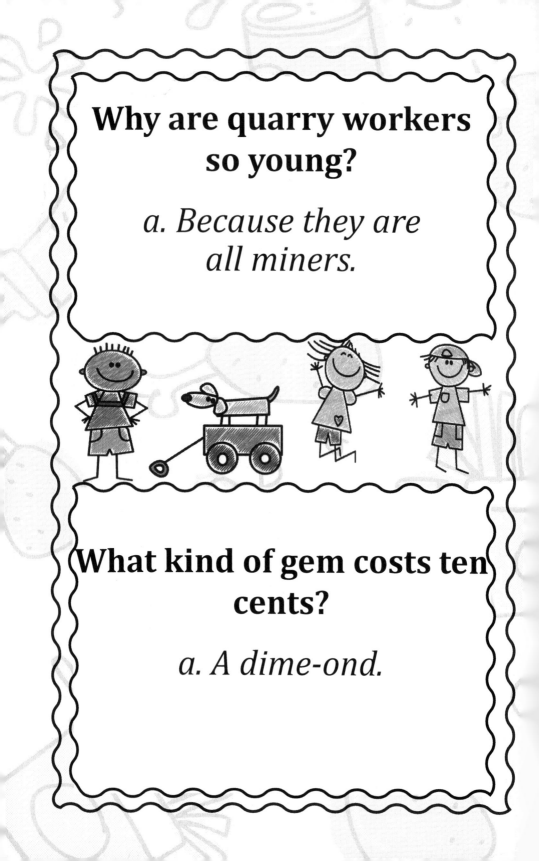

What kind of gem costs ten cents?

a. A dime-ond.

Kid: This flower doesn't smell like anything.

a. That doesn't make any scents!

Why couldn't the cow afford a car?

a. Because it cost too much mooney.

What did the angry rabbit say to his friends?

a. "You don't carrot all!"

What do you say when you leave a store with a great purchase.

a. "Good buy!"

What did the bee call his wife?

a. Honey.

What animal smells bad?

a. Any animal without a nose.

What does a shark say when it's done eating?

a. Fin-ished!

Why should a karate expert not join the army?

a. Because if he salutes he'd give himself a head injury.

What kind of bulb isn't heavy?

a. A light bulb.

How did the insect get into the concert?

a. With its tick-et.

Where do the best lawyer's compete?

a. At the sue-per bowl.

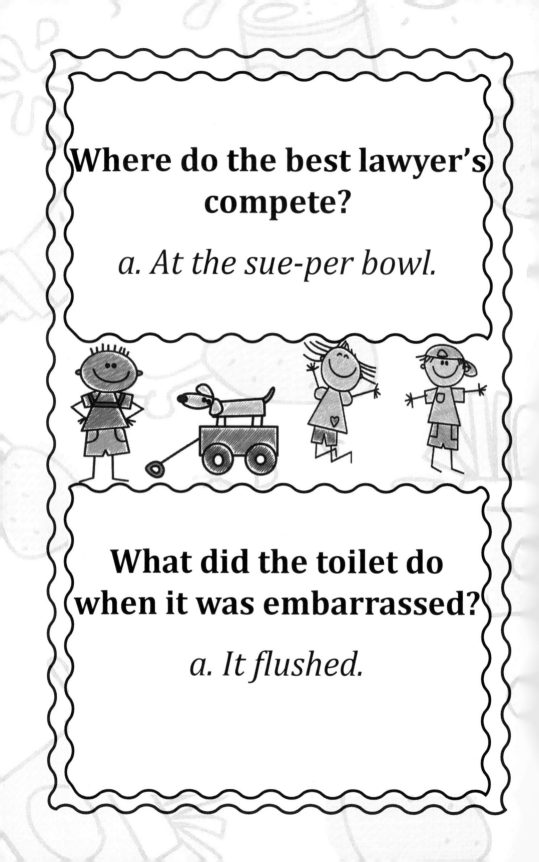

What did the toilet do when it was embarrassed?

a. It flushed.

What do you call a man inside a paper bag?

a. Russell.

How do you line up canoes?

a. In rows.

How did Jupiter propose to Saturn?

a. By giving it a ring.

Why was the king ten inches tall?

a. Because he was a ruler.

What does the buck call his sweetheart?

a. Deer.

What kind of dog is the best to guard your boat?

a. A docks-und.

What do you call it when Saint Nicholas goes to the beach?

a. Sandy Claus.

What is the most musical fish?

a. *Tuna fish.*

What is a cow's favorite lunch meat?

a. Bull-ogna.

How do you do a survey about phones?

a. Take a telephone poll.

What is the coldest blanket?

a. A blanket of snow.

What does a snowman do when he goes to bed?

a. He drifts to sleep.

How does a whale cry?

a. It blubbers.

What's worse than finding a worm in your apple?

a. Finding half a worm in your apple.

When is long shorter than short?

a. When you're counting the number of letters.

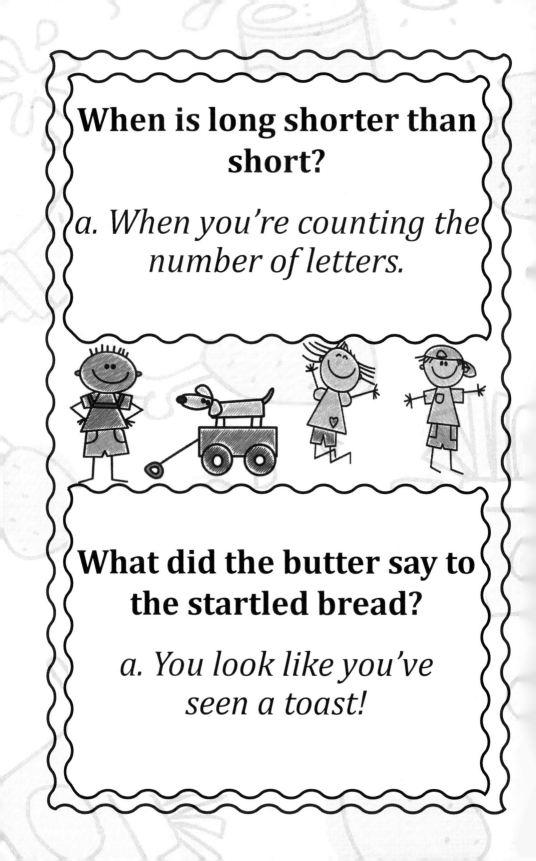

What did the butter say to the startled bread?

a. You look like you've seen a toast!

What are the best shoes for bakers?

a. Loafers.

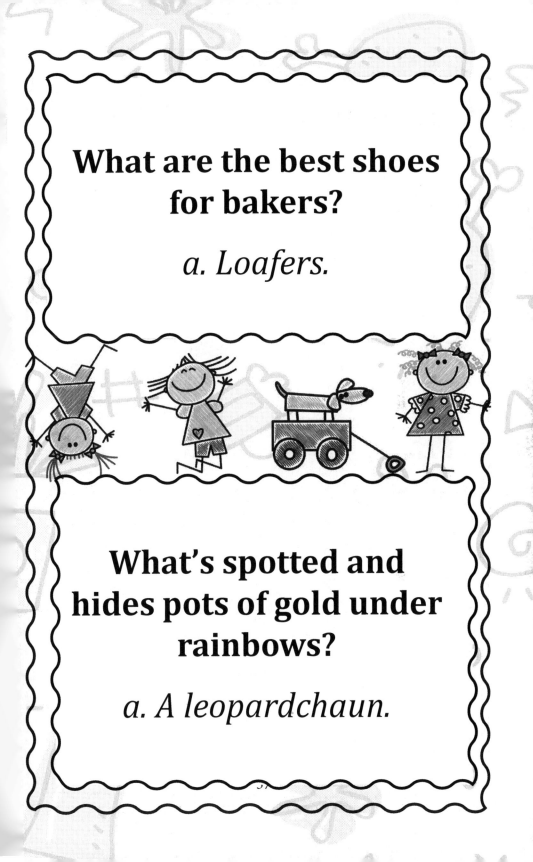

What's spotted and hides pots of gold under rainbows?

a. A leopardchaun.

What do you give an Australian when he wins a chess tournament?

a. A check, mate!

Knock knock.
a. Who's there?
b. Noah.
c. Noah who?
d. Noah good restaurant around here?

Knock knock.
a. Who's there?
b. Claire.
c. Claire who?
**d. Claire out of the way,
I'm coming in!**

Knock knock.
a. Who's there?
b. Mikey.
c. Mikey who?
**d. Mikey doesn't work.
Could you unlock the
door?**

Knock knock.
a. Who's there?
b. Figs.
c. Figs who?
d. Could you figs the doorbell? It doesn't work!

Knock knock.
a. Who's there?
b. Dozen.
c. Dozen who?
d. Dozen anyone want to let me in?

Knock knock.
a. Who's there?
b. Olive.
c. Olive who?
d. Aw, I love you too!

Knock knock.
a. Who's there?
b. Imma.
c. Imma who?
d. Imma freeze if you don't let me in soon!

Knock knock.
a. Who's there?

b. Roach.

c. Roach who?

d. Roach you that I was coming. Did you get the letter?

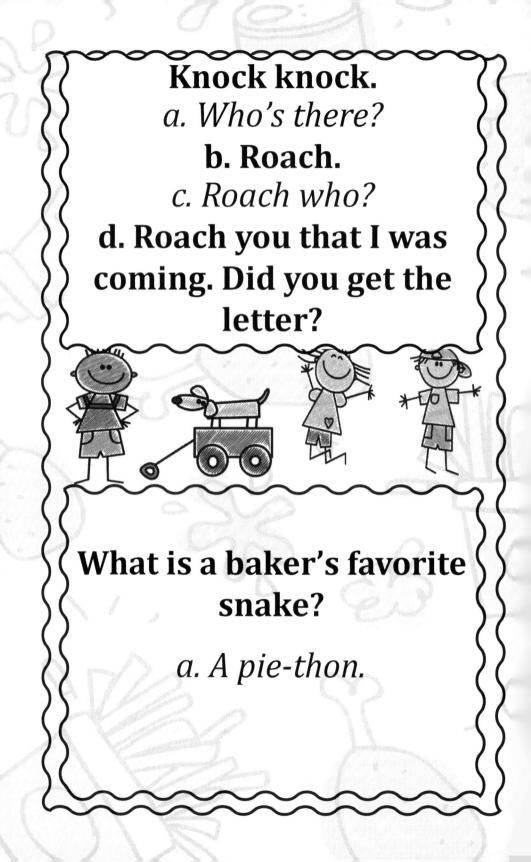

What is a baker's favorite snake?

a. A pie-thon.

Why was the doctor so mad?

a. Because he ran out of patients.

What state has the tiniest beverages?

a. Mini-soda.

What does an alien play when he's driving to work?

a. Nep-tunes.

Why did the baseball player get arrested?

a. Because he stole a base.

Where did Cinderella go to eat bacon?

a. To the meat-ball.

Why are mountains so good at comedy?

a. Because they're hill-arious.

Why are chickens so good at being in bands?

a. Because they have drumsticks.

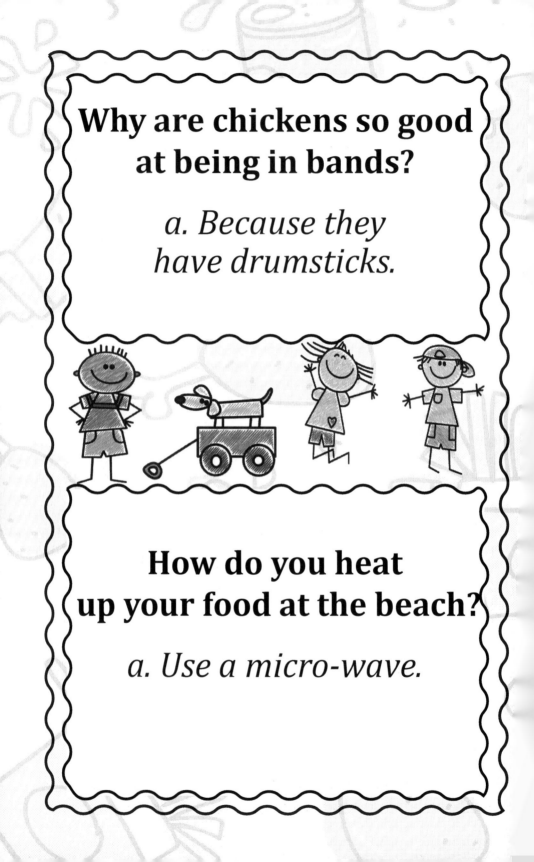

How do you heat up your food at the beach?

a. Use a micro-wave.

Where do you learn how to make ice cream?

a. At sundae school.

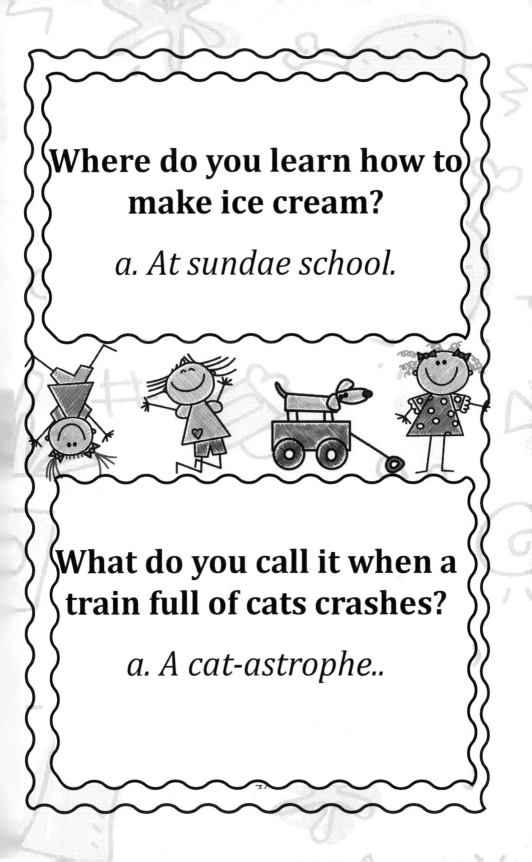

What do you call it when a train full of cats crashes?

a. A cat-astrophe..

Where do sheep get their haircut?

a. At the baa-baa shop.

What do cows do for fun?

a. They go to the mooooovies.

Why did the flower go to the dentist?

a. To get a root canal.

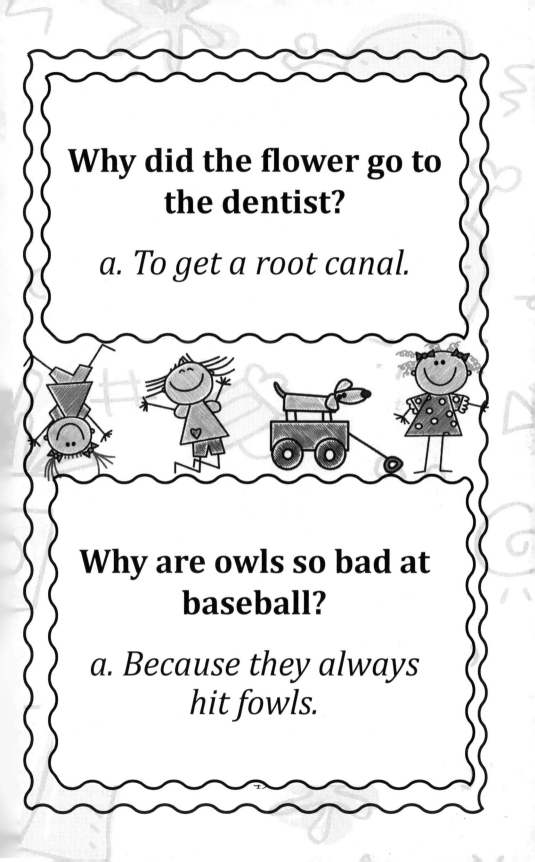

Why are owls so bad at baseball?

a. Because they always hit fowls.

Why do carnivores like moon rocks better than Earth rocks?

a. Because they're meteor.

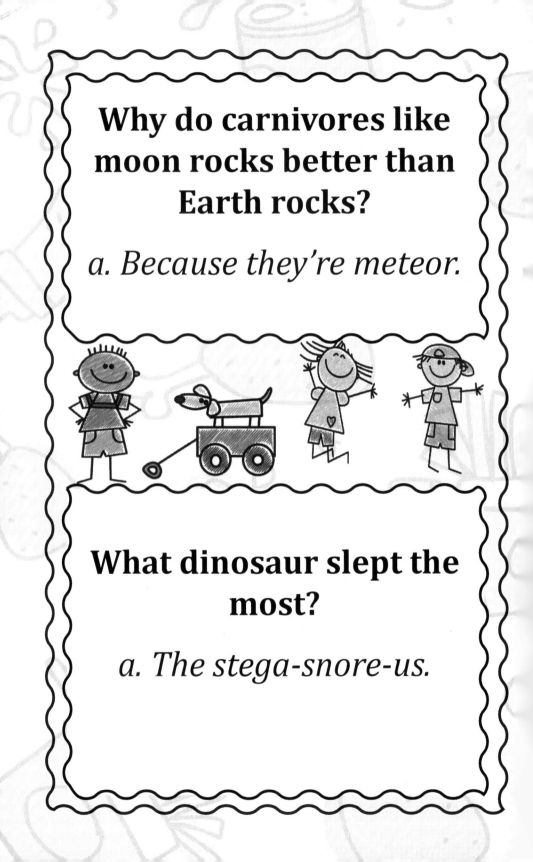

What dinosaur slept the most?

a. The stega-snore-us.

Why did the moon stop eating?

a. Because it was full.

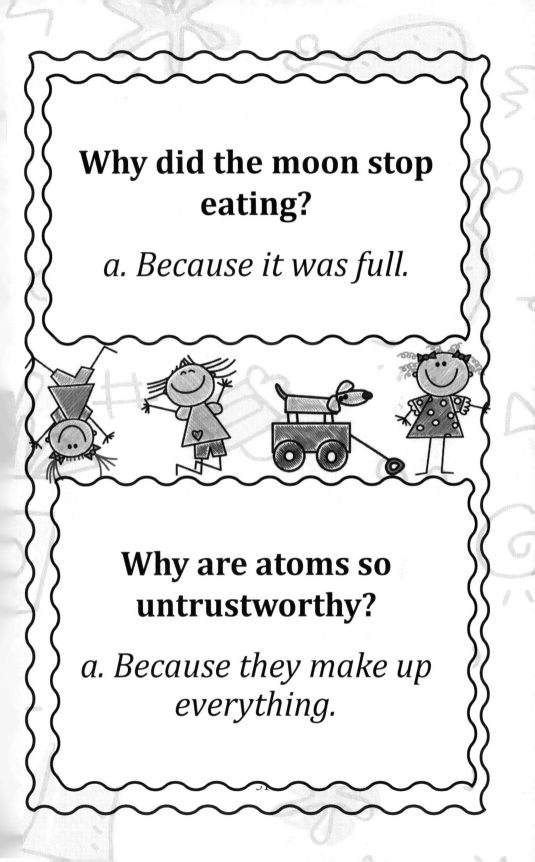

Why are atoms so untrustworthy?

a. Because they make up everything.

Made in the USA
Columbia, SC
19 June 2019